CW01391332

7 Nov 2024.

<u>To</u>: Steve,

To many 'happy'
money - making
years together.

Mariette.

FREE THE HIDDEN SPEAKER INSIDE

HOW YOUR VOICE CAN MAKE YOU MONEY & GIVE YOU THE LIFE YOU DESIRE

MARIETTE RICHARDSON

©Mariette Richardson 2020
This edition published: November 2020 by FCM Publishing

ISBN: 9781838091828 Paperback Edition

For Johan Cloete

*Dad, thank you for putting me
on a chair when I was three and
encouraging me to speak*

Speakers are made, not born

— MARIETTE RICHARDSON

ACKNOWLEDGEMENTS

If it hadn't been for my publisher, Taryn's encouragement and guidance, this book would not have been a reality. Thank you, Taryn. Proofreader, Sarah is a true professional. You made the book so easy to read, thank you Sarah. Jan turned a manuscript into a beautiful book, thanks.

Melanie, Hendrik, Claire and Elsa, thank you for sharing your wisdom with us. And to my clients for allowing me to share their questions and anecdotes. Stephen, my business mentor, who had to 'force' me to stop rewriting and get it done! I owe my success to you. My producer, Dave, thank you for believing in me. Michelle and George, your support is greatly appreciated.

My friends and family – Bets Basson, my mentor, and my three sons and three daughters, you keep me going. And then to the most kind-hearted and patient man under the sun, Carl, thank you for loving me the way I am. I could not have done it without you.

CONTENTS

2

STEP TWO: **DON'T TALK, ENTERTAIN**

3

STEP THREE: **DON'T WALK, STRIDE**

OUTPERFORM
YOUR PEERS

IN THREE EASY STEPS

THE THREE STEPS

ONE: LOOK THE PART
TWO: DON'T TALK: ENTERTAIN
THREE: DON'T WALK: STRIDE!

1

STEP ONE:
LOOK THE PART

Do you want to be a presenter? Do you want that job? Do you want your voice to earn you money? Well, you'd better start to look like a presenter, walk like a presenter, speak like a presenter, eat like a presenter, think like a presenter and most certainly, act like a presenter.

Your voice is your way to success. The way you communicate – not just when you are present-ing – is what gives you the edge, ensures your next promotion, clinches the next deal or lets you blend into the background and become part of the furniture.

I hear you say:
"But I don't want to be a presenter. I've been put in this job and it's required of me to present, whether I like it or not!"

You're not alone. You work hard at learning your trade, you put in extra hours to achieve the highest grades, but have you been taught to promote yourself?

If only we could go back to being that confident little kid in the playground who proudly boasts that "*My dad is stronger than your dad*" or "*My house is bigger than your house*!" It's only when we grow up that we become self-conscious and inhibited.

Simon, a young graduate with great expectations, finished his degree right in the middle of the financial crisis of 2008. After applying for jobs for a full year, he realised that nobody was hiring. Out of desperation he took a job in a factory and worked without pay for three months.

In his third month, his boss got promoted and Simon anticipated that he might be considered for the vacant position. One day his boss called him in. "*Young man look at this*," he said. He put three CVs in front of him. One was from an applicant with twenty-two years' experience, the next one had fifteen years' experience and although number three had only seven years' experience, he was the best qualified.

Simon said he felt as if his whole life was about to implode. He was totally broke. He was in a strange city with no family or friends. If he didn't get that job, he'd be sleeping on the streets.

He felt as if he was drowning. He lowered his head, his shoulders slumped and for a moment it felt as if he was going to faint. Then he fought back the tears and said in the strongest voice he could possibly muster: "Mr Smith, if I had seven years' experience, I wouldn't be applying for this vacancy – I'd be applying for your job!"

Simon only got the job because he opened his mouth and spoke up. It took a huge amount of courage, but it paid off and today he is an accomplished speaker in a highly paid position.

Follow my three rules to become a memorable speaker on screen, on stage, in boardrooms and sales meetings.

RULE NUMBER ONE: LOOK THE PART

> *"If you want to do business,*
> *you better look prosperous."*
> — COCO CHANEL

Style consultant Claire Mathews says:

"When you look in the mirror and smile, you'll know that you've got 'The Look'."

'The Look' also refers to the way you carry yourself, your body language, your stance and ultimately the complete package that you present to the world. I'm still baffled by the impact my shoes can have on the way I feel. Even when I'm participating in an online meeting, I feel much more confident and in control when I'm wearing good shoes. You can get away with wearing slippers, but a pair of Louboutins will definitely give you a lift (no pun intended).

You might have heard of the seven percent rule. Albert Mehrabian in his book *Silent Messages* (1971) says that his research proves that fifty-five percent of a speaker's body language determines the success of their sales pitch and another thirty-eight percent depends on the tone of their voice. Mehrabian received criticism from various sources – mainly due to the fact that he based his findings on a relatively small sample of thirty undergraduate women. To claim that ninety-three percent of a speaker's success is down to non-verbal signals does seem a bit high, I agree. However, Mehrabian still deserves credit for recognising that body language plays a significant role in our communications.

Looking prosperous matters when you're meeting with clients in person while networking or attending conferences. However, it can still add to the impact you make on a prospective client if you tidy up a bit before a video call. You just need to make an extra effort with your appearance beforehand. Comb your hair, wear a clean shirt and brush your teeth.

Brush my teeth? Yes, even the smallest detail like unsightly food particles will affect your performance. By brushing your teeth and rinsing your mouth, you'll also ensure a clean and open speech passage. People do strange things with their lips, tongue and jaw when under stress: they bite or purse their lips, chew or suck their tongues or stick their jaws out unnaturally. And if there is a tiny food particle in your mouth, you will constantly roll your tongue to try and free it without realising what you're doing. By rinsing your mouth, you have taken the first step towards clear speech. You've made it possible for the sound to glide smoothly and unhindered through your voice passage, right to the farthest corners of the room.

If you exert yourself just a tiny bit more than usual, you are saying to your audience:
"I respect you, so I've spent time and energy to look my best for you."

CAN MY VOICE MAKE MONEY FOR ME?

Try to make money without a voice. No, seriously! From the moment you speak, the quality of your voice and your appearance matter far more than what you're actually saying. You might say:

"Hang on, I've been preparing and rehearsing my presentation for weeks and I know that I've chosen my words well."

Good for you! But if you deliver that meticulously compiled presentation in a wavering voice – and your body language conveys to your audience that you're uncomfortable – then you might as well sit down.

While networking recently, when I introduced myself as a voice consultant who coaches people in public speaking, someone said to me: "*I never do public speaking.*" I calmly asked him: "*Sir, do you speak and do you go out in public?*" Every time you encounter a person in public and start up a conversation, you are performing some form of public speaking. You are using your voice to convey a message, to convince, influence or educate another person or a group of people, whether your audience consists of one, one hundred or one thousand – the only difference will be the equipment you use to address your audience. The true professional is the one who can speak to a million people as if he is only talking to one.

Never underestimate the impact of a beautifully modulated voice which is resonant, rich and perfectly pitched – it immediately commands attention and respect. You will be amazed at how much you will grow in stature when you master the art of speaking: you will be able to open your mouth and grab people's attention purely with the sound of your voice.

Public speaking is not a hobby;
it is the foundation of success.

BE YOURSELF

Parents, teachers and bosses find it easy to say:
"*Stand tall. Be bold, speak up. You can do it.*"

But what happens if you can't? If you simply
don't have it in you to stand in front of an audience and speak with confidence?

How often have you felt unworthy, a failure, at a
loss, timid or insecure? Even though you may be
very successful, I bet there are still times when
these thoughts overwhelm you. Celebrities, who
always look beautiful, have a lot of help to enable
them to appear well-groomed in public. Who do
you have in the morning when you wake up and
look in the wardrobe? How do you know which
outfit to choose and which colour suits you?

The two people in the photos on the next page
have been shortlisted for the position of brand

manager at a growing concern in London. Which one will you appoint?

There, I caught you! The mere fact that you participated in this exercise proves that we judge by appearances. Without knowing anything about these two candidates, you were prepared to make a decision. Cruel? Indeed, but that is human nature. To add insult to injury, the moment you open your mouth you are further judged.

What should you do to make a favourable impression?

Look like a presenter…

WHAT DOES A PRESENTER LOOK LIKE?

A presenter has authority, is respected, can be trusted, instils hope and exudes confidence and credibility. You might think "*that's not me*" – and if you do you're certainly not alone. According to Professor Jeffrey R Strawn from the University of Cincinnati, seventy-five percent of all humans suffer from glossophobia – the fear of public speaking.

Numerous polls name public speaking as the worst fear of all. The fear of death is in fifth place and loneliness in seventh.

That's exactly the point. You aren't afraid of the actual speaking, what you fear is the judgement – the age-old phobia of not being good enough. When you have to speak in public, you're suddenly all alone and in full view of an audience. From the moment you get up from your chair and walk forward to take your place, you are being scrutinised from the crown of your head to the tips of your shoes. This might not actually be true, but it feels as if everybody is judging you. An online meeting may be worse, as you're constantly aware of your image on screen and this can be nerve-wracking.

The irony is that everyone in the meeting is there for their own selfish reasons. They are there because it's cool to be part of a team, or they want to impress their boss, or they think it's important to network. Besides that, they are thinking first and foremost about themselves: tomorrow's presentation that still needs tweaking; the nice man or woman they flirted with in the pub last night; their child's soccer game and so on. You're just another person who walks onto the stage with a speech which might interest them – or not. That's the reality.

The fear is in your head not theirs. They will of course form an impression of you – and yes, they will judge you – but not in the same way that they'll judge a celebrity such as Justin Bieber or Meghan Markle.

TONGUE POWER

Audiences are, on the whole, rather forgiving and quite compassionate. Probably because thirty people in a room of forty (seventy-five percent) will look at you on that stage and think: *"Wow, I could never do that!"* You assume they'll judge you, when thirty of them might actually admire you. Therefore, if you see yourself as one of the ten percent of people who do speak successfully in public, you will confidently walk forward to face your audience – no matter how big. And if you experience a dry throat, nausea or shortness of breath, say to your body: "*Thank you for the adrenaline, partner. I need it.*" Then walk – no, stride – up there and give it your best shot! You're not going to be scorned or ridiculed; you'll gain respect and recognition. That's when you'll succeed in turning your glossophobia into glossodunamis – tongue power.

Having said that, many introverts are almost paralysed when it's their turn to stand up and talk. I call them 'The Chosen' because, ultimately, they'll become better speakers than extroverts. Why? Because everything they say is more meaningful, they don't try to impress and are never arrogant. But they do tend to speak quite quickly. One of my clients made me laugh when he said:

"I speak so fast because I just want to get the whole thing over with as soon as possible!"

Speaking in public is like learning to ride a bicycle – you will fall off, you will lose your balance, but one day you'll suddenly find your rhythm and begin to enjoy the ride. I've been reciting on Eisteddfod stages since the age of six and I still suffer from stage fright, but once I'm there and I've said my first three words, I always settle down. My knees often start to shake when I walk off and sit down, but that's fine – it's only the final spurt of adrenaline.

Applause is highly addictive because it gives us immediate gratification. It satisfies our deepest need to be recognised: to be seen, to be known, to be famous and rich. My aim is to make you look forward to your next public performance. Don't fear it, enjoy it.

The moment you make an effort to start looking like a presenter you'll begin to feel like one – and soon you'll believe that you are one. It begins with '*The Look*'. Let's start to look like speakers.

NUMBER ONE: GET FIT

Nutritionist Melanie Ryan says the brain consumes twenty percent of all our energy – which means, as a speaker you're going to think on your feet and focus one hundred percent – and in the process think yourself slim. Well, the research hasn't confirmed my theory just yet, but it's certainly going to keep you occupied and away from the fridge.

You have to begin by asking yourself these three questions:

- How serious am I about winning?
- What stops me from succeeding?
- What does my body look like?

I don't have to tell you how important the answers are… the mirror will.

I can teach you all about voice production and delivery techniques, content compilation, visual aids and how to use a microphone, but it'll all be to no avail if you don't look like a speaker. By that I don't mean that you have to be six feet tall and look like Luke Evans or have hair like Kate, the Duchess of Cambridge, but you will need to work at coming across as well-groomed, fit, healthy and happy in your skin. You'll need to look like an influencer even if you aren't one... yet.

NUMBER TWO: EAT LIKE A SPEAKER

If you want to maintain cognitive and mental strength, it's not enough just to eat brain food – you also need to eat at the right time.

I rehearsed with someone who was going to present a workshop the following day and our session started at three o'clock in the afternoon. After only ten minutes I realised that her energy was fading, so I interrupted myself and asked her what she'd eaten today.

"Um, well, a banana for breakfast, a cream scone for tea and a pasta salad for lunch," she replied.

Did you know that what you eat can make speaking engagements much easier? From the time you get up and start walking to the speaking area, your audience is busy forming their first impression. Is your step a little sluggish? Does your whole demeanour suggest a lack of energy? If this is the case, it may not be that you aren't putting enough hours in at the gym. It's more likely that you're eating the wrong kind of food at the wrong time of day.

If you want to feel like a speaker and look like a speaker, then you're going to want to follow a balanced diet that will provide you with the right amount of energy when you need it most. This reminds me of Christo Gerlach, a TV director who became a legend in his own lifetime, who always shouted into the presenters' earpieces: "*Energy, energy, I want energy!*" Don't be a wilted lettuce leaf – make sure you feel energetic on the day of your appearance.

WHAT SHOULD I EAT AND WHEN?

You need protein and it's best to have it at least three hours before your presentation. Protein provides sustained energy which enables you to present your ending with the same high-spirited enthusiasm as your opening.

Do you find it hard to get out of bed in the morning? Are you hungry not long after breakfast and succumbing to your mid-afternoon slump every day? Does a snack and coffee helpfully prop you up when required? That's how most of us get through the day. And yet, in the long run, this way of eating is not helpful at all. It depletes our energy rather than supplying it. It contributes to stress and, over time, even to insulin resistance, diabetes and heart disease. You're on a blood sugar rollercoaster.

The afternoon slump or 'two-thirty feeling'
is largely due to your circadian rhythm,
a twenty-four hour 'master clock' that
regulates hormones in your brain. Worst
of all, your audience is also experiencing it,
therefore you'll need to exude extra energy
to gain their attention and hold it. The best
natural energy booster is peppermint tea or
a minty mouthwash, which also serves to
clean your speech canal. Maybe you should
hand round some peppermints!

Your blood sugar spikes five or six times each day, only to crash again shortly afterwards. No wonder you might feel tired at a time when you need your energy the most! But there is another way.

If you want a steady energy supply and not feel tired all the time, try this:

- Cut out sugar including molasses, honey, maple syrup, agave syrup, and anything ending in 'ose' like lactose or fructose.
- Fill half your plate with non-starchy vegetables (greens, cauliflower, peppers, asparagus and leeks), a quarter with protein and the remaining quarter with low-GL starchy food.
- Fresh and frozen fruit is an excellent source of vitamins and minerals, but also a source of sugar. Tropical fruits, such as pineapples, mangoes and bananas, tend to be higher in sugar than fruit that grows in higher latitudes such as berries, cherries, plums and apples. Dried fruit is very high in sugar and affects your blood sugar just as much as regular sugar and should therefore be avoided.

ON THE DAY OF YOUR PERFORMANCE

Eat

If you get nervous before speaking in public, you may find that nerves have ruined your appetite, but it's still not a good idea to go out there on an empty stomach. Note that sugary foods may supply immediate energy, but the high is invariably followed by a low so don't be tempted to grab a slice of cake or a banana just before your performance. Such foods, alas, seem to be readily available at many conferences. Keep your blood sugar even at all times by following a low-GL or low-carb diet.

Drink

On the day of your performance, choose drinks that are at room temperature or, better still, at body temperature. An ice-cold drink can cause the muscles in your throat to constrict, whereas a drink that is too hot, can burn the roof of your mouth or hard palate. Avoid sugary drinks too – they tend to cause phlegm.

Alcohol

Alcohol can dry out your throat and tongue and make your voice hoarse. Moreover, alcoholic drinks – especially cocktails – are often high in sugar. Even worse is when you arrive at the venue with the smell of alcohol on your breath – consider what the organiser might think and is it the first impression you want to make?

Dairy

Dairy products include milk, yoghurt, cream, kefir, butter and cheese. When milk mixes with saliva in the mouth, it can create a feeling of thickening saliva and phlegm. If you feel that dairy affects you in that way, avoid it on the day of a performance. If you've never noticed any impediment, then you're one of the lucky ones who does not suffer from mucus formation caused by dairy.

Heartburn

Heartburn or acid reflux is extremely common. When stomach acid touches the bottom of the oesophagus – which it shouldn't – it causes a burning sensation and sometimes a sour taste in the mouth. It can also be accompanied by burping or audible tummy rumblings – which I call the 'gastric symphony'. This is certainly not something you would want to experience while speaking into a microphone! The best way to prevent tummy rumblings, is a good breakfast and a light snack at least two hours before your meeting.

Caffeine
Studies performed by the School of Sport and Exercise Sciences at Loughborough University in the UK have proved that caffeine has a mild diuretic effect. Be careful, that cup of coffee could make you want to run to the toilet as your name is called.

Overhydration

If you need to urinate a lot, it could be because you are drinking too much. Your urine should be the colour of straw. If it looks more like apple juice, then you need to drink more fluids. If it's clear, you could be drinking more water than you need. Remember that smoothies, salad and fruit also contain fluids.

The Lung Health Institute (lunginstitute. com) named these foods as the most common mucus triggers: red meat, dairy, eggs, gluten, bananas, potatoes, soy, sugar, caffeine and alcohol.

DO I REALLY NEED TO LOOK THE PART?

No, you don't. It's not a prerequisite for a successful public appearance, but it certainly goes a long way to improving your confidence and self-esteem and that's why I highly recommend it.

Most of us don't know where to start to find our look. That's when an image consultant can not only save you time and money, but also educate you in terms of your body shape and style personality.

Popular image consultant Claire Mathews says: "*Looking the part is not buying what is displayed on a mannequin in a store; what is ever so tempting in an online brochure; what somebody else is wearing walking down the street or copying what your friends are doing – it's about 'you doing you'. Quite often we don't know how to do that. An image consultant's job is to strip away the excess and guide you to look at your body, your personality, your style and how we can make the best of you. You need to connect with your clothes.*"

When doing business, you want to be standing in your own power. Claire uses the analogy of King Henry VIII and how a soldier under his reign would present himself. He would wear a hat – in our case, that relates to our hair. Is it neat and tidy? Does it suit the shape of your face? Maybe a bald head is your most complementary look. If you are naturally more relaxed and easy-going, you may need a free-flowing style with a bit more texture. Then we come to the jacket and the shoulder detail: are our shoulders too rounded or do we need shoulder pads? Shoulder pads would make you appear taller and slimmer. Have you got wide hips? Do we need to crop the jacket so that it does not sit on the widest point of your body? A soldier would have carried his armour on his belt and a belt – especially in business – is still a statement piece. It makes us come across as authoritative and professional. And it makes the audience think: "*Who is this person? Let me hear what they have to say.*"

Claire believes that wearing a watch actually says to the other person: "*I respect your time.*" Being on time for a meeting is absolutely vital. Things sometimes go wrong and that's life however, allowing yourself enough time to pitch up goes a long way towards creating a positive first impression. For a virtual presentation, you should join at least three minutes before the meeting starts. That brings us to necklines which are especially important in online communication.

Coming back to your body shape: if you have soft curves in your body, you should shy away from angular lines around your neck. Choose a scooped neck or softer collar line instead. Gentlemen who wear ties need to think about the design: a funky rose may complement your curved body shape more than sharp stripes or diagonal shapes. By taking note of these so-called minor details, you are honouring yourself and at the same time sending out an authentic message that "*this is me, this is my look, and I'm presenting my best to you*". One of my friends never leaves the house with socks that match – his trademark is two different colourful socks. Why not?

Claire goes on to explain how either blue or yellow fat cells in the epidermis of the skin, seem to illuminate or come forward when she drapes a colour swatch over a client's shoulders. If you're wearing the wrong shade for your skin type, your skin will appear quite poorly, sickly and sallow. Your cameo area or communication zone – eyes, mouth, cheeks and jaw – will almost disappear. Your eyes will lose their specific hue, your lips will look pale and your jawline could appear to change shape. You could even gain weight! The circles under your eyes may appear darker and your skin could look patchy. Skin problems like rosacea and acne will be highlighted. The colour you place directly under your chin can make all the difference.

More importantly, colour enhances your mood and that in turn stimulates productivity and performance. Richard Branson clothed his Virgin Airline staff from head to toe in true red. It's one of the most appealing colours to the eye and, more importantly, it conveys the subliminal message of *"I'm in charge, I know what I'm doing, I'll take care of you"*. Wear the colour that best complements you and step into your power.

NO STRANGERS IN YOUR WARDROBE

What if a person's budget does not allow for an image consultant?

"Save up! Because you save money in the long run," Claire explains. *"Stop for a moment and think: how does this outfit make me feel? Did I buy this because it served a purpose or because it will do? But now when I try it on, I have no real connection*

to it. You need to feel good when you put an outfit on. Do your clothes make you smile? You don't need any strangers in your wardrobe."

Appearance is not dictated by the amount of money you spend. It's about how you wear your clothes and care for your hair, teeth and nails, but what's most important is how you carry your head on your shoulders.

MY LOOK MANTRA

When you have an important speaking event, this should be your mantra: clean, tidy and smashing! By smashing I mean wearing at least one item that will steal the show – shoes, scarf, hairstyle or jewellery. Something that is dear to you and that gives you that edge. You know what I'm talking about. Even if it's the jacket you bought ten years ago, if you still feel good in it then wear it.

The idea is to feel comfortable and it begins with your shoes. Whatever you do, try to avoid wearing new shoes. They might pinch, squeak, they might even cause you to trip because you are not used to them. Choose the good old standbys: the ones so comfortable that you're not even aware of them when you put them on.

Seven tips for looking successful and credible:

1. Monotone colours always work. Neutrals pair well with anything and never go out of fashion and then you add the surprise element: something in an accent colour.

2. Good quality fabrics are essential because they keep their shape and look smart for longer.

3. Underwear makes all the difference! It does not only contour your body, but it also gives you that extra oomph that only you know about!

4. Think in threes: one is your main garment, two is your shoes and three is the wow factor – that added element of surprise that puts you in a different class. For a man it could be his designer socks.

5. Tailoring is the secret; perfectly tailored clothes make you stand tall and speak up with conviction.

6. Discover your best look. I recommend the assistance of a professional stylist, but if that is beyond your budget then ask the one friend who has always been brutally honest with you. Set a day aside and go through your cupboard. Don't get upset, listen to what he or she has to say and throw things out! It's better to have ten outfits you love than a hundred collecting dust.

7. Lastly, your nails should always be clean and manicured – that goes for men as well. Your hair should be healthy, shiny and neat and your lips should be moist. Ladies, never go into battle without your mascara and lipstick. And for the men, beeswax cures dry lips and will stop you from licking them.

Beware of shiny jewellery and fabrics that catch the light and may cause beautiful dancing lights or even rainbows over the audience. You won't realise it, but your audience will look at the rainbows and won't hear a word you're saying.

When I invested in an image consultant, the real eye-opener was when she pinpointed my style personality. It made all the difference and her male clients, she assured me, echoed that. The moment you know what your true image is, you begin to live up to it. You become that personality and suddenly it not only changes the way you perceive yourself, but also the way you present yourself to the world.

WILL GOOD TEETH MAKE ME SPEAK BETTER?

"People who have a lovely smile talk to the world in a different way."
– DR HENDRIK FREEKE

Absolutely! We don't realise how our teeth impact our overall appearance, confidence and pronunciation. We marvelled at how Rami Malek became Freddie Mercury in *Bohemian Rhapsody* – not an easy feat for any actor – but his real breakthrough came when he finally mastered speaking and singing with the upper teeth prosthetic made especially for this role.

If you're not blessed with a beautiful smile, the investment you make in your teeth may be one of the best business start-up expenditure decisions you've ever made. Dr Hendrik Freeke, a leading cosmetic dentist in the UK, says:

"*The perfect smile consists of perfectly aligned teeth, a 1.5 mm overlap of the upper teeth over the lower teeth, nice big arches – the width of the jaw as well as the height of the palate – and all the teeth facing forward and not rotated towards the back. For me, Liz Hurley has the ideal smile.*"

When the cutting edge of the front teeth is too far backwards, it's impossible to pronounce sounds like *f*. When the dental arch is too narrow, meaning the teeth are too close from side to side, you won't be able to put your tongue forward enough to pronounce *s, sh, t* and *l* sounds. Julia Roberts, for example, has a very wide dental arch compared to Hugh Grant, who has a narrow arch.

Hendrik has a severe problem with parents who say to their children: "*Don't worry, darling, your crooked teeth add to your character.*" Or "*Mummy loves that little gap between your front teeth!*" In his opinion you're not doing your child a favour. That endearing gap may mean that some people never smile, which changes their whole persona. Hendrik says:

"The good news is that once your teeth are aligned, they will last longer without any further intervention. If they are positioned incorrectly, they automatically grind each other down. We subconsciously grind our teeth to try and get rid of those irritating edges that are protruding in the wrong places."

A simple procedure like tooth whitening, which is a fairly inexpensive treatment, will go a long way towards increasing your self-confidence. Hendrik tells the story of a dentist in America who treated a contestant in a beauty pageant. One of her front teeth appeared grey compared to the rest. The dentist simply corrected the rotation of the tooth so that the light reflected in such a way that its colour changed from grey to white! Needless to say, she went on to win the crown.

Be warned: red wine, black tea, black coffee, curry, turmeric and betel nuts will stain your teeth. Your only option will be a thorough session with a dental hygienist who'll use an ultrasonic instrument to remove the discolouring.

AND HAVE YOU HEARD OF A DENTAL FACELIFT?

Beauty editor and blogger Elsa Krüger writes: *"When looking at your smile from the front of your face, your doctor wants to see a hundred percent of the front two teeth, then sixty-six percent of the side two."* This ratio continues towards the back of your mouth. Dental Facelifting is an intricate process, however, by merely bringing the tooth length back to where it was during adolescence, a more youthful appearance can be achieved.

Something that I found most interesting when reading her blog, is that the colour of the teeth is determined by matching it to the white of the eye! Which goes to show that a healthy lifestyle resulting in a healthy glow, sparkling teeth and bright eyes, not only makes you feel like a speaker, but also ensures that you look like one.

ZOOMING OUR HEARTS OUT

As we are communicating remotely more and more, it's important to understand correct camera and microphone techniques.

Remember: you need only to smile at a networking meeting and you're on Twitter. That's why celebs are super-conscious about how they look, act and smile. Being on Camera and in the public eye is unavoidable. But that's good, isn't it? It's free promotion on our behalf and we should use it to our advantage – by embracing it and being 'videoable' at all times.

By the way, I'm writing Camera with a capital C because the sooner you make the Camera your partner, the sooner you'll gain the necessary confidence to embrace your online presence. Okay, I understand that not everyone has the urge to be photographed. Many of my clients have admitted that they shy away from photoshoots and would rather die than appear on TV. On the other hand, some extroverts dream of being on TV.

One client was asked to participate in a television show to demonstrate the use of their gin infusions. Although he dreaded it at first, afterwards he said that he enjoyed it so much that he was looking forward to the next one. As soon as you manage to forget about the Camera and only focus on what you're saying, your nervousness will subside, and you'll begin to enjoy it. And, of course, the more you enjoy yourself the more the viewers will enjoy it too.

MAKING LOVE TO THE CAMERA

Best framing

How you position yourself in front of your camera is of the utmost importance. Your face or body forms part of a complete picture, so your background is equally important. People are very tolerant if you're working from home, but you're certainly going to make a better impression during a job interview if you're not sitting against a glare and your background is tidy and neat. Never sit against a door frame – you might look as if you have been framed!

Flat background

A bare wall behind you might look neat, but it's very unforgiving because there is nothing in the background to soften or round off your image. You are completely exposed. Every twitch, every hair strand that is out of place, every crease is highlighted. A background with some depth creates a much more pleasant setting, which makes you also come across as inviting and friendly instead of formal and distant.

Camera height

The camera should be at eye level or slightly above. When you look slightly upwards, you'll open your eyes more and lift your chin, which will make you come across as younger – a great help if we believe the old adage that the camera adds ten pounds to your weight and seven years to your age. The cardinal sin is to look down into your camera from above so that we end up peering into your nostrils! Apologies, that sounds crude, but lighting guru Angus Clarke says it is the bane of his life. The 'up the nostrils' shot doesn't do anybody any favours.

Talk to one person

Always visualise a single person at the other end of the camera and not the masses. Most of us do a video recording as if we are addressing an audience of thousands, but that is totally wrong. One person is going to watch you at a time and the moment you change your mindset to address that one specific person, you'll be amazed at how much more intimate, personal and ultimately credible your presentation will be. That person needs to feel that you have prepared your message solely for him or her.

Looking into a camera

Here is the trick: never ever look at the camera – look through it. Think of the camera as a conduit – a passage through which you can see the person on the other side. Try filming yourself looking at something opposed to looking through it and you'll notice that your gaze actually looks completely different. Looking at something easily comes across as staring, whereas looking through something makes your eyes seem inviting and you come across as confident and engaging.

Styling

The camera prefers a simple look. To quote Angus Clarke again:

"*Choice of clothing is very important as it detracts the centre of attention from the face, which completes the actual communication loop.*"

Opt for plain colours and avoid busy patterned fabric. Multi-coloured designs are particularly distracting on camera. Clothing in darker colours, such as navy and charcoal are preferable to white tops which easily 'burn out' under lighting, especially against a darker skin. Colours that are dangerous on camera are pastels because they will appear washed out, any psychedelic colour and sometimes yellow. Avoid green at all costs in case you end up shooting against a green screen.

Strobing

Some fabrics cause psychedelic patterns on a screen; it almost looks as if a tie with small dots is dancing when one watches it on TV. Avoid tiny patterns such as checks, dots, narrow lines or houndstooth. Even the loosely woven fabric of a coat or jacket can appear to strobe on camera. Do a pre-take test, video yourself and play it back on your screen to make sure that you are safe.

Hair and makeup

We always joked in broadcasting studios about the amount of time it takes to do hair and makeup, but if you take into account that the presenters and actors filming close-ups are literally under a magnifying glass, you can appreciate how important it is that your hair should be smooth and tidy. Make-up hides skin blemishes and translucent powder masks excessive sweating.

Radio mic

In a broadcasting studio and any filming situation, you will probably use a mic. A lapel or radio mic is a wonderful aid; however, it needs to be respected. Do not touch it under any circumstances. If you have long hair, make sure that your hair does not brush against it, check that the collar of your jacket or your scarf does not cover it and if you use a cue card or water bottle, don't bump the mic accidentally. It's imperative that you do a proper sound check before recording.

Desk top mic

The most important thing is to make sure that you are at least eight to twelve inches away from the microphone. When you are too close, you might cause the microphone to distort and popping might occur – when plosive sounds like *p* and *b* are overemphasised.

Background

Make sure that nothing grows out of your head – that there isn't, for example, a standing lamp or potted plant directly behind you which looks as if it's sprouting out of your ear.

Position yourself in such a way that you are facing the natural source of light. If you're video calling at night, avoid sitting directly under a ceiling light because it will cause unsightly shadows under your eyes and nose. The best lighting for a face is level with your eyes from the front, with one light on either side to eliminate shadows.

2

STEP TWO:
DON'T TALK, ENTERTAIN

Early one morning, in the spring of 1931, Coco Chanel set sail for America. Hollywood mogul Samuel Goldwyn had invited her to meet his female stars to design outfits for them for their upcoming movies. But first she was going to meet with the board of directors at Macy's, the big departmental store in New York, to persuade them to stock her new perfume, Chanel No 5.

The board turned her down. With her head held high, she walked to the top of the big marble staircase right in the centre of the store and 'accidentally' dropped a huge bottle of Chanel No 5. The loud bang rang through the stillness of the building as the bottle shattered into a million pieces... then slowly the magnificent fragrance drifted through the entire store.

Women from all over rushed up to her, shouting: "What is it? Where can we buy it?" To which Chanel replied: "Soon, chères mesdames, it'll be available in this very store."

Everybody talks, but very few people make an impression. If you want to be heard, I suggest you forget about preparing a speech and prepare to entertain.

I can hear you protesting: "*I'm not a storyteller, I'm not an actor.*" You don't need to be an actor to entertain, but I'm telling you that you'll have to come up with something creative if you want to be noticed.

To entertain means addressing people's emotions. You either scare them, upset them, infuriate them, make them laugh or make them sad... if you can elicit a tear, so much the better. Donald Trump learnt this lesson long ago and goes out of his way to be outrageous. You don't have to be a comedian, but you do need to step out of your comfort zone and give your audience something to talk about.

I know the accountants are now rolling their eyes and thinking: "*Entertain? Who, me? I'm not a clown!*" You're right and that's the last thing you should try because it will seem fake. However, have you considered opening your presentation with a short anecdote which captures the essence of the budget? If it's something personal, it will have a much greater impact. By letting them into your personal life – even if it's telling them how you staggered on the Tube and landed on a lady's lap – you convey to them: "*Hi guys, I'm normal, I'm one of you, you can trust me.*" As soon as you allow them to identify with you, it'll put them at ease and help you to relax and enjoy the time you spend with them as well.

People relate to stories. Sketch a situation which they can identify with and you'd be surprised by the reaction. Your audience will suddenly grow quiet and listen.

Communications expert and renowned actor Bill Brand puts it like this:
"*Instead of projecting, listen. Instead of commanding attention, draw attention by giving attention.*"

He even refers to public speaking as "*public offering*". I like that. You are not here to speak to people; you have been given the opportunity to offer a group of geniuses something that may enrich their already brilliant minds. Something that they did not know. If you want to bore them, give them facts and figures that they can google themselves.

Even if you are delivering a financial report, you can package it in a way that is unique and personal. Perhaps your boss doesn't allow you to change anything, but you are still the person who has been chosen to present the report. Let your personality shine through.

Put yourself in your audience's shoes. What are they interested in? How can you help them? One of the best speeches I've heard was made by Phil Berg from Business Network International. He said: "*Our parents taught us not to talk to...*" and of course the whole audience shouted out: "*Strangers!*" He replied: "*I say: talk to strangers!*"

I remember his speech to this day, and I've shared and reshared this exchange many times. Why? Because he entertained us. We joined in, we laughed, we had a bit of fun during a rather drawn-out morning. By bringing in some light-heartedness, his presentation stood out far above the rest.

Learn from Phil. Leave them with one thing they'll remember, and they'll go out and say to their colleagues: "*He's a terrific speaker!*" Even if you aren't, by stirring their emotions you gave them something to tweet about.

HOW TO TURN A GOOD VOICE INTO A GREAT VOICE

Audibility does not need to depend on the use of a microphone. In fact, you have your own built in microphone – those unique resonators which enable you to project loudly and clearly without straining your voice. You'll be amazed at how much confidence and presence you'll gain once you've learnt how to access it.

Voice placement, or the art of projection, is an intricate and highly specialised technique taught by performance professionals in an in-depth voice enhancing course. For the purpose of this book, I can explain it simply by saying that the voice needs to be released from the throat and brought forward into the mouth. The mouth is the chamber where the sound is enriched and amplified.

If you say "*t-t-tttt*" you will feel how the tip of your tongue drums lightly on the hard palate directly behind your upper teeth, that is where you should 'taste' your words. This is what I make my clients say over and over again: "*Taste the words on the tip of my tongue.*" And the secret is to actually taste your words on the tip of your tongue.

Here are some basic voice exercises you can do in the bathroom or the car as long as you don't look sideways to the person stopping at the traffic light next to you! They not only enable clear pronunciation, the process also tightens facial muscles, which is certainly a plus.

- Releasing tension in the neck: Stand upright, create space between ears and shoulders. Rub your hands together to create energy and then massage your neck muscles while counting to ten. Slowly and gently drop your head forwards and count to five, now backwards for five counts – take care not to strain it. Put your right hand on your head; don't pull, simply let it rest, so that the weight of your arm gently stretches the muscle. Do the same to the other side.
- To loosen the jaw: Yawn with an open mouth for at least five counts, longer if possible. If

you experience any discomfort, begin by doing smaller yawns and only open your mouth wider as your jaw becomes more re-laxed.

- Purse the lips and smile as broadly as possible. Do this at least ten times.

- Stick your tongue out as far as possible, curl it back along your hard palate making sure that the tip of your tongue is tightly pointed. When you reach the back, you'll feel as though you need to swallow.

- Push your tongue into your right cheek as far as you can – in fact you should try and push it right through your cheek. Now to the left, repeat the movements at least ten times. Your tongue will probably hurt. If it does, just suck it for a few seconds to relax it. Any discomfort proves that your tongue muscles are stiff and need some stretching.

Once you have mastered the art of producing a rich and strong voice, you will open your mouth and people will listen to you. To reach that level requires professional guidance and perseverance from your side, but once you've accomplished it your whole life will change. Just imagine how your confidence will soar when you can rest assured that people will always hear you – even in an auditorium without a microphone. No one will say "*pardon*", "*say that again*" or "*sorry, I can't hear you*". The moment you speak in a clear, beautifully resonant voice, you'll come across as authoritative, convincing and trustworthy.

The sound of your voice is crucial to the impression you make. People listen first and foremost to how your voice sounds before they hear what you are saying. If you hear the voice on the other side of the phone saying hello, you will immediately form a picture of the person behind that voice, is that not so? If you phone your mother, she only needs to say hello and you know immediately what mood she's in. And that's even more relevant when you're speaking to your boss! Our voices give away so much of our mental and physical wellbeing, as well as our stress levels, that it's almost impossible to disguise our feelings when speaking. Just think how many criminals have been caught because their voices gave them away.

I'm in awe of voices. Each one of the approximately eight billion people on earth has a unique voice – which of course led to voice recognition technology.

What contributes to your specific voice quality are factors like your parents' way of speaking and the way their voices are placed and formed; your teachers and friends and their way of speaking which you subconsciously copy; the structure of your voice box and vocal folds and, more importantly, how you access your resonance cavities.

The female voice is normally higher pitched because her vocal folds are shorter and thinner than that of her male counterpart. During puberty boys produce a surge of testosterone which causes their vocal cords to elongate and thicken – thus producing a deeper sound.

LISTEN TO YOURSELF

In order for you to better your speaking skills, it is imperative that you start listening to yourself and become aware of the sound of your own voice. How fast are you speaking? How soft or how loud? How clear is your pronunciation? Are you mumbling? Is your voice monotone?

Record a voice note and listen to it, try to distance yourself from the person speaking and dissect it phrase by phrase. Can you hear every word? Does this person complete his words, or does he tend to swallow the last words in a sentence or stumble over the last syllables of words?

Here is a fun exercise to do: page through any magazine and choose an advertisement. Begin by marking the pauses in the copy or text, draw a single line like this / for a short pause; // for a medium pause and /// for a longer pause and a small tick ∧ between words where you think you should just pause slightly.

The beauty of a pause – which I call, my 'little miracle worker' – is that it gives you instant variation, clarity and emphasis in your speech. It forces you to think about which words are important, which ones you should lightly skip over to reach the important one and which words should really stand out.

Look at this last phrase, if I were to mark it, I'd do the following:

"...and ∧which words / should ∧really // stand out."

The use of pauses differs from person to person and is certainly a definitive characteristic of our unique way of speaking. By the way, you should never try to copy anybody else. Retain your personal speaking style: your only aim should be to correct obvious problem areas such as inaudibility, a too fast tempo and mumbling.

Do the advertisement reading exercise and you'll understand what I mean about becoming aware of pauses. You'll soon realise what a pause can do to put your audience at ease and, in the process, put yourself much more at ease. Think about it: your audience has to listen to what you're saying, take it in, process it and visualise it before they can understand it and retain that thought. Give them time – it's almost impossible to pause too long.

Oh, yes, I forgot to mention something! The moment you feel that you are losing your audience – and as a speaker you know exactly what I mean, when you pick up that the audience is not with you – the best way to regain their attention is to keep quiet. Teachers have been applying this trick for ages. They simply keep quiet and look at the class – and it works. The moment you stop talking, you'll have their full attention, which means you should definitely pause before the one line or thought that you want them to remember. Make it a palpable, throbbing, alive pause and you will hold them in the palm of your hand. They will stop breathing and wait for your next words. Pauses and body language go hand in hand.

There is a difference between a 'live' and a 'dead' pause. A dead pause is when you simply don't talk. A live pause is when you don't speak, but your body is still communicating.

Remember, you don't just communicate with your voice or with your words – you also communicate with your whole body. Your feet communicate: do they stand still or are they constantly taking inconsequential little steps forwards, backwards, sideways to the left and the right like an amateur boxer at his first boxing lesson? Stop! The moment you start dancing around, your body is telling us that you are nervous and – even worse – you are projecting that uneasiness onto us and soon we will start to shift in our seats. I've even witnessed some audience members getting up and leave because the speaker made them feel too jittery!

The way you carry your head on your shoulders, how you place your feet and how you take ownership of your performance area, are the factors that say: "Take note, this is going to impact your life." Rehearse in front of a full-length mirror or record a video selfie; only then will you realise how much you are saying without saying a word.

A speaker must come across as grounded. The more grounded you are, the more in control you will seem and the more we will be able to trust, believe and respect you.

Try this: move your weight towards your heels. When your weight is placed on your toes, you will feel slightly off balance, but you will feel a lot more stable when you focus on standing firmly on your heels. Ladies who wear high heels will need to make an even more concerted effort to appear grounded.

WALK AND TALK

You don't have to stand still when you make a speech, in fact you'll come across as far more relaxed and at ease if you use your speaking area to the full. Movement adds interest and you'll find it easier to interact with your audience if you take a few steps towards them while speaking. If you use a projector, just be careful not to become a human screen.

I encourage speakers to move. Movement creates interest, brings a valuable change in your presentation and communicates to your audience: "I'm confident, trustworthy and speak with authority." You might be on a stage where the lighting engineer has instructed you to stay behind the lectern (lecterns are my worst enemies, I'll explain why later), if so, please negotiate with him to give you a bigger spotlight which will allow you at least a bit of freedom to move.

The secret is to walk and stand, walk and stand. Take a few steps forward, to the side, approach your audience and narrow the gap between yourself and them by walking closer to them if your speaking area allows it – but always adhere to the rule of walk and stand, walk and stand. And don't be afraid to turn your back on your audience. The purists are certainly frowning now: "*Back to audience? Never!*" I say: try it and just see how empowered it makes you feel.

Just imagine the suspense you'll create if you put a question to the audience and, while you wait for someone to respond, you pause, turn your back on them, walk a few steps back and then spin around and look at them – wow! If that doesn't spur them on to react, nothing will.

Always remember the rule: take a step or two or three, then stand still (totally grounded), until you are ready for your next move.

As a speaker you should own your speaking area. The moment you accomplish that, your presentation will progress to the next level. This is your stage, therefore, you have the right to move around it as you feel. The more relaxed and in control you seem, the more your audience will relax and enjoy it.

MAKE AN ENTRANCE

Your presentation begins the very moment that you stand up to walk forward, the second you appear into sight from backstage or join a virtual meeting. Prepare yourself physically before you start.

Here's the recipe for walking onto a stage or speaking area:

Step one:
Begin by creating space between ears and shoulders, then move your weight to your heels.

Step two:
Breathe in two, three, four – hold, two, three, four – out two, three, four – stay two, three, four. 'Stay' means relax without breathing to the count of four. This is one of the best relaxation exercises I can give you. It takes your mind off the task ahead and, if you count silently in

your head, nobody will even notice that you're breathing rhythmically.

Step three:
Take your water bottle, laptop if it is not already set up, cue card or any other prop you may need such as a clicker and walk towards your speaking area purposefully and energetically. Your body should say: *"Hi, I'm excited to present this message to you. You're going to love it."*

Step four:
You have memorised your first three to five words. Look your audience in the eye and say them in the strongest voice that you can muster.

When getting up at any venue and walking to the front, this recipe will apply:

Step one:
Create space between your shoulders and ears.

Step two:
Stand up in one slick move, grab hold of the back of the chair and push your one leg against the seat of the chair – then simply take one step back. Voilà! Your chair is now sufficiently out of the way for you to move away without tripping over it. Remember to make sure that there is room behind you before you push your chair back. I have been in crowded meeting rooms where I had to step sideways away from my chair. You might need to stand up, walk around your chair and push it under the table to get out, or you may choose to stand behind it and start speaking from there!

Another excellent tip is to start speaking the moment you begin to walk to the front. You have immediately gained attention by being different from the rest: you've sparked their interest. Anything goes as long as you are in control, relaxed and self-assured.

Your entrance when you join an online meeting requires the same presence from you – look up, create space between your ears and shoulders, make eye-contact, smile if it's appropriate and react with energy and positivity.

Your opening will make or break you. Once you've heard your voice travelling strong and secure across the room or over the speakers in an online meeting, you will not believe what a tremendous confidence booster that is.

Always know your first five words off by heart. That's the only way to fly out of the blocks – to set the pace for a victorious performance. Your whole performance depends on those first three to five words – as the Scottish football coach and former player, Lee McCulloch, said: "A flying start is key to success."

WHAT DOES YOUR SPEAKING AREA OFFER YOU?

Another important point is to look around you and use what is available in your speaking area. One client chose to talk about Elon Musk when I asked him to do an impromptu speech about his role model. He began by talking about what he admired most about Elon: *"I admire his ability to challenge everyone around him to think out of the box. He certainly does not make us feel safe,"* he said. Directly behind him on the wall was a slogan, as part of the boardroom decorations, which stated: *"We keep you safe."* At the right moment, he turned around, pointed to the slogan and said: *"By keeping us safe, dear board members, you'll never produce more Elons!"*

What an ending! I was thrilled that he applied my advice and used his space as part of his speech. If there happens to be a ladder backstage, bring it onto your speaking area and climb up a few steps to illustrate your point of looking at life from a different angle, or use it as a stand for your notes and water bottle. You can also peep through it to make a point. I know what you're thinking: *"I'm not a comedian!"* No, you're not, but you will make your speech more memorable if you can come up with a creative idea to make your presentation stand out.

One of my clients was asked to do a presentation about the advantages of contracting an interior decorator. She was the keynote speaker at the opening of an interior shop and the presentation was going to take place during the opening ceremony. Can you imagine the challenges? People were going to be milling around, having drinks and snacks and evidently talking. We cut her talk down from thirty minutes to ten and got rid of the slides, so it became a demonstration rather than a presentation. We made use of the furniture in the shop. She chose one armchair and dressed it in three different ways. By adding different lamps, she gave tips on lighting and discussed briefly the importance of lighting in a room. She involved the audience by asking them which rugs or cushions they liked and showed them how to add them creatively. What could have been a disastrous speech turned out to be a highly entertaining and informative workshop. And it was profitable too: she gained two clients and the shop sold two chairs!

That brings me to one of my pet peeves: lecterns. Especially if it's one of those heavy brown furniture jobs. It cuts you in half and if you're short we'll barely see your head! If you have to stand behind it, make sure that you can rest your arms on it easily. The lectern should not be higher than your elbows. If it's any higher than that, you should ask for a stool, box or even a few books to stand on. I always have my folding stool in the boot of my car, just in case.

As you know, we talk with our whole bodies. Your stance, your arms, your legs, your feet – every part of you contributes to making that crucial overall impression and ultimately getting your message across. Engage with your audience by leaning towards them and you'll be surprised at the effect it has on them. Always request a radio mic which will give you the freedom to move away from the podium and walk around the stage or speaking area.

CENTRE AND FLAT ANGLE

Another handy tip, which is equally important when taking your stance in your speaking area or when you position yourself in front of your device camera, is to angle your body slightly to the left or right. Photographers know how much more appealing the human body and face appear on camera if they are slightly angled and not positioned exactly straight on.

When communicating remotely, you do not have to sit slap bang in the middle of the screen. Move a fraction to the side and angle your body ever so slightly to see what a difference it makes. You'll look more in control, friendlier, inviting and trustworthy.

SCREW IT!

When presenting, a water bottle is not just a cure for a ticklish throat – it also serves as a prop. Greta Thunberg certainly convinced me to throw away my plastic bottle. However, if you're still using one then make sure it's not the thin crackly type, but one with a good, solid base so that it will stand firmly when you place it down. And I recommend a screw top, because it allows

you three extra seconds to unscrew it – three precious seconds you'll be thankful for if you need a moment to gather your thoughts when your mind goes blank.

Use your bottle in exactly the same way as you would in the gym. Take a sip, gesture with it, hold it, move it from one hand to another. Put it down, pick it up, unscrew the top, take a sip, then put the screw top back on and place it on the table or chair next to you. By doing this, you've gained that little bit of extra time to regain your confidence.

Another handy prop is your clicker – with newly replaced batteries, remember. It gives you something else to do with your hands. And, finally, cue cards. My belief is that every good speaker should use notes. It conveys a positive and professional message to your audience, it says: "*I took the trouble to prepare well, I value you, I respect your time.*" Cue cards should never be hidden. Display them openly and also use them as a prop to gesture with, to refer to openly and handle them with confidence. Just make sure that they are neat, small enough and numbered. Should you drop them – which happens regularly – you can easily place them in the correct sequence again.

You should never have more than five cue cards, one for every level of the Pyramid Method of building a presentation (see image on the next page). I prefer my phone, iPad or laptop as a means of cueing, but technology has a way of letting us down at the most crucial moment. I once had my cue words on my phone and the moment I looked at it, a call came through! The secret of course is to switch it to airplane mode. Therefore, a set of printed cue cards as a backup might not be a bad idea – at least their batteries won't run flat.

HOW TO COMPILE A PRESENTATION

I first came up with the idea of a pyramid when I realised that most clients don't know where to begin when compiling a presentation, speech or elevator pitch. If I should ask you: "What is your speech about?" and you reply by saying: "Trees and their role in saving the human race from extinction." That would be the essence of your message – level three of the pyramid – and that is where you should begin to prepare. In a sales pitch, it's the key element that is going to clinch the deal. In an annual report, it's the wow factor: this year's exciting news that is going to instil renewed interest in the company.

Pyramid Model

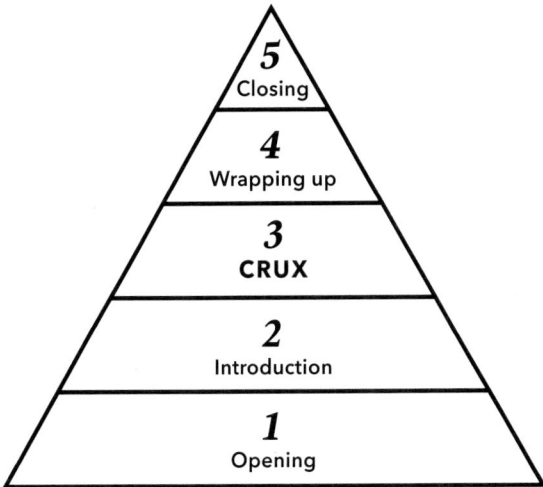

Then go to level two – the introduction to your core message. Keep this short, perhaps use an ice breaker or ask your audience a question. Level two is also a good place to create suspense, i.e. "This has been a tough year, however we found a solution... be patient, I'll soon tell you more."

We now go on to prepare level four – time to start winding up, maybe tell your audience how they can apply what you've said on level three.

Now it's time to think of your opening - the foundation of the pyramid. Be bold, be creative, be different. Grab their attention instantaneously.

I usually leave level five until the last. This is your opportunity to bowl them over - it's your Instagrammable moment and what your audience will tweet. You might have heard the expression, "leave them laughing", which television producers swear by. Leave your audience feeling good about themselves, leave them on a positive note so that they'll walk away saying: "What a good speaker!"

Opening no-no's:

■ **Thank you** – *Thank you for inviting me; thank you for the opportunity; thank you for your time.* No, you don't have to thank us, we need to thank you for coming to share your expertise with us.

■ **I hope** – *I hope you'll enjoy my presentation; I hope to share some insightful truths with you tonight; I hope you'll take home some new ideas.* The moment you say 'hope', you convey to the audience that you don't believe that you can deliver an enjoyable or insightful presentation.

- **I'm sorry** – *Please forgive me for being late; this is the first time that I've done this; I haven't had time to prepare.* Don't ever apologise, especially in your opening.

- **Good evening** – *Good evening, ladies and gentlemen.* This is a boring, over-used and unimaginative opening and please don't ever add: "How are you?" If your audience does not respond, you'll have to repeat your question and might get a weak answer from two or three people. You'll end up with egg on your face and, in the process, you've ruined your first impression.

- **So or okay** – These are stop words people use the moment they feel self-conscious. In my book, they're definite no's. And I often hear a combination of the two: "Okay, so…!"

Opening yeses:

- **Stories or anecdotes** – My favourite type of opening! People are intrigued by stories – could it be because it takes us back to our childhood? We grow quiet and listen the moment we realise that someone is about to tell us a story.

- **Questions** – "*Are you one of those people who wears twenty percent of your outfits eighty percent of the time?*" An interesting question my stylist friend, Claire Mathews, used as an opening. Questions or quotes can work extremely well.

- **Something else besides words** – When you open with a visual aid or prop – maybe an object, an image, a movie clip, a piece of music, an architectural drawing or a child's painting – your audience will sit up and take notice. You are different and you thought outside the box.

- **Arresting facts** – If you can open with surprising facts or statistics – something that addresses the emotions of your audience – you'll immediately create interest.

- **An announcement or promise** – By announcing that a prize will be awarded at the end of the evening, you'll create interest and hook your audience in. Maybe only tease them in the opening and keep the surprise for last.

Closing no-no's:

- **Thank you** – Definitely not.

- **Goodbye and good night** — You are not the Master of Ceremonies. In fact, I'd advise him to think of something more original too!

- **That's it from me then** – Need I say more?

- **Time for me to go** – You don't need to say that, simply finish and walk off graciously.

Closing yeses:

- **Summary** – Summarise your speech in one clear phrase, reiterating the single most important thought.

- **Quote** – A suitable quote can be a good ending.

- **Anecdote or story** – An anecdote always works: *"I'd like to leave you with..."*

- **Pinpoint an incident** – Pick up on something that occurred during your presentation, i.e. after an online meeting: *"We've had phones ringing, dogs barking, dishwashers going and coffee machines gurgling – you've truly made me feel at home. Thanks, team! Next week: same time, same place!"*

WRITE A FULL STOP WITH YOUR VOICE

The trick is to say your last words as if it is the end. Pause slightly before your last important word and then write a full stop with your voice. Let your voice drop in pitch (not in volume though) and make it clear to your audience that this is the end. Keep looking at them, count to two in your head, then bow your head slightly and walk off or sit down. The idea is to let your last words sink in before you look away or rush off. If they applaud – which I'm sure they will – you simply smile, bow your head slightly, smile again and start walking off. If they encore or clap louder, you can graciously smile and come back and say, *"You're a great audience, I'm definitely coming back!"* Or follow your instincts and say what your heart tells you.

The same applies to communicating virtually, again write a full stop by using a pause and lower your pitch. Look into the camera, count to two, and only then shift your gaze or move.

You may say to yourself: *"I'll feel like a fool staring into the camera like that!"* I can assure you; you'll create a much more professional image than your colleagues who look away before or on their last word!

YOUR POEM IS INSIDE YOU

My very first performance teacher, Sheila Shlain, taught me a valuable lesson which has stood the test of time. She gave the class a new poem to learn and we were instructed to take it home and illustrate it. In week two, we had to come and tell her the story of the poem in our own words. By week three, we discussed the poem with her, and she told us more about the poet and his background. We began to dissect the poem in week four and she discussed its structure and rhythm. Only in week five were we allowed to read it to her. When we finally began to learn the words in week six it came naturally. By internalising the content first, it was much easier to perform it.

When you do a presentation in your field of expertise, your poem is already inside of you. However, you need to trust yourself. Often when a client is too dependent on their notes and I ask them to turn off their laptops and tell me, as a novice, what the presentation is about. They're always surprised by how much they can say without a single note in front of them. When you begin to trust your knowledge more, you won't have to use your slides as notes. You'll be able to use them as a visual aid to enhance your presentation.

If your presentation falls outside your field of expertise, you should internalise it first. Move in with it, sleep with it, dream about it and literally live with it. I can hear you saying: "*I don't have six weeks to prepare, I barely have six days.*" In the real world six weeks' preparation time is a luxury, so you need to rely even more heavily on your poem and use anecdotes from your life to spark interest. One morning when I was making my way to a net-working meeting, I saw a team of workers who just completed the installation of a huge sign above a new business. As I stopped at the traffic light, they pushed the ladder away and turned on the lights. "*Stardust*" glittered and sparkled in bright daylight. Their smiles said it all. I shared that experience in my elevator pitch and said: "*You should leave your audience with at least one 'stardust' moment.*" Then I started to tell what I had seen.

If you truly understand what you're saying, your thoughts will flow effortlessly.

IMPROMPTU SPEAKERS... HOW DO THEY DO IT?

Easy! They use their poems. If you are asked to speak off the cuff, begin by linking the subject to something that you've experienced, heard about or read. You know what they say? Don't tell a story as it is, tell it as it should be – and since you're telling them about your poem, poetic licence might be in order, not so? Mark Twain was right when he said: "*It usually takes me more than three weeks to prepare a good impromptu speech.*"

HOW DO I REHEARSE?

If you are a relatively inexperienced presenter, it may be sensible to write out your speech in full, but I wouldn't recommend memorising it word for word. In fact, I want to go so far as to say I forbid you to memorise your speech! You'll concentrate so hard on remembering the script that your delivery will end up sounding stilted and insincere. I would strongly advise that you choose some key words, the fewer the better, and put your full speech to one side. The Pyramid Method makes it very easy to extract five key words, one main key word for every level and maybe a few secondary ones. I suggest you mark the five main key words in red, which will make it very easy to remind you on which level you are and what to talk about next. The poem analogy also applies here. You know what you want to say, so your cue card is only your satnav, pointing out where to go next.

You'll notice that every time you do the presentation, it will differ slightly, and that's perfectly fine as long as you think about the meaning of what you're saying and speak from the heart. I prefer to rehearse in front of a full-length mirror in my bedroom with the door closed. I know some of you might think it is wise to ask your partner, wife or daughter to rehearse with you, but I find any person who is close to you is often a worse critic than a group of strangers.

Rehearse your movements as well as your gestures. Don't stand still. Take control of your space. Take a step to the left and look to that side of the audience. Look them in the eye, engage with them, then move to the right and engage with that part of the room.

By the way, 'death by PowerPoint' is not a joke. Ten slides are far too many. You need a powerful opening slide; a creative icebreaker – a visual that will make them sit up. Then four or five informative slides to illustrate your point and a closing slide which reiterates your core message.

Refrain from reciting your whole speech on the way to the venue. It will only confuse you and, if you get it wrong, it might freak you out so much that you become agitated. Trust yourself. Your speech is inside of you. You are prepared. You have rehearsed and you have your notes to hand. When you are on stage, it will come back. Now is the time to relax, give yourself a break, listen to music and switch off.

WHAT DO I DO WITH MY HANDS?

This is one of the questions I get most frequently and that's understandable. Our hands seem big and get in the way when we're speaking to a camera, while our arms feel extra-long when we're standing in front of an audience! Do we fold them? Hide them behind our backs? Let them hang by our sides? No, use them! Easier said than done? Definitely, here's my advice.

I recommend that you lock your elbows into your waist and let your hands come together naturally. There! You are now in a comfortable position to move your arms about freely. Try relaxing one arm by your side while gesturing with the other or you may prefer to use both hands in unison.

The rule is rather fewer, big and open gestures than a myriad of small, inconsequential, worthless gestures which have no voice. Treat your hands as you'd treat a visual aid: they should emphasise what you're saying and not compete with your message.

Our hands give us away. A person who does not use gestures at all comes across as stiff, guarded and unapproachable, whereas someone who presents himself with open shoulders, open hands and strong, definite gestures, immediately gains trust because he displays the image of someone who's in control. The audience will immediately pick up that you're nervous when you start to fidget by touching your hair or smoothing your clothing. Even a tiny gesture like tapping your fingers together can become totally distracting if you repeat it more than twice.

To get back to hands, when communicating virtually the secret is to sit further away from your device. Lift your screen to match your natural eyeline and consider tilting your screen slightly forwards to show more of your body. Your eyes should be in the upper third of the screen. There you go! Now we can see more of your shoulders and your hands won't appear too big. Finally, your way of gesturing is unique to you. Don't change it, just remember that fewer and bigger movements are more effective than repetitive fluttering, which soon becomes irritating.

And one last tip: I would advise you not to fold your arms or put your hands in your pockets. By doing this your body language says: "*I'm bored; not interested; in a hurry or disgruntled.*"

HOW TO HANDLE A MISHAP

Once on a long-haul flight, our captain greeted us with:

"*Good evening, ladies and gentlemen, my name is Peter, I'm your captain on this flight and I'm now happy to leave you in the capable hands of one of my favourite cabin managers...*"

Silence. Our captain couldn't remember the name of his favourite cabin manager. There was a roar of laughter, but still not a word from our captain. It was the perfect opportunity for him to have gained our admiration if he managed to come back with something like:

"*John Smith, of course. I can assure you, ladies and gentlemen, I can fly better than I can remember names.*"

Look out for those little gems along the way – those unexpected moments that present the ideal opportunity to come up with a creative quip that will make a lasting impression. Use it in such a way that the audience will think you've actually planned it. For example, on another occasion our captain said:

"Good evening, ladies and gentlemen, I've had a complaint from a passenger that one of our tyres seems to be exceptionally smooth. I want to put your mind at rest, sir, we are going by air and not by road!"

As long as you don't try and ignore an interruption or mishap! That won't do because your audience has also seen or heard it, therefore, it is far better to acknowledge it and use it to your advantage. If a person storms into the boardroom in the middle of your presentation, you could say: *"You've made it! Come and join us."* One of the ways to handle a phone that suddenly starts ringing, is to say: *"Perfect timing! Please answer and put us on speaker."* And if you're presenting in a virtual meeting and one of your kids decide that they need to walk past to the kitchen, you could say: *"These extras, I've told them to wait for my cue."*

If you're looking for the right word to use, then ask. Never be ashamed to ask your audience. If you show them your human side, it will surely endear you to them.

SPEAKERS SHOULD BE SEEN AND HEARD

Always position yourself opposite the source of natural light. If you are doing a sales pitch, it will be to your advantage if you are facing the window and your opponent is sitting with his back to the window, because that automatically places him in the weaker position – unless you actually want to scrutinise his facial expressions, then by all means put him in the light.

If you are in a meeting room with no windows and there is a ceiling light above you, the trick is to take one step back or sideways so that the light falls on your face from an angle.

As mentioned, the ideal lighting for a face is at eye level from both sides, so most shadows will be eliminated. However, as a speaker, you are not always able to dictate the lighting at a venue. Therefore, you have to work with what you've got: optimise natural light sources and position yourself in such a way that the available electric lights shine on you from sideways and from the front – not too high and not too low. And please request that TV screens – or any unnecessary screens that are not utilised to enhance your presentation – are switched off. You certainly do not want to compete with moving images and disturbing light flashes behind you.

This is your moment, embrace it and step confidently into the spotlight.

GET IT RIGHT THE FIRST TIME

Do you know what the ultimate confidence killer is? A faulty microphone. It immediately conveys one message to the audience: unprofessional. And there goes your first impression – and you know why they call it a first impression? Because you have only one chance to make it. If you come back and ask to start your presentation again the audience will, in most cases, humour you. However, the second time around will be your second impression and you cannot erase the impression they've already formed of you.

You might think that's cruel. It's even more cruel when you consider that you've only got three seconds to make that first impression. It goes like this: one – they see you; two – they form an impression of you; and three – they judge you. Then you get either a yes or a no.

I've heard about a billionaire businessman from Dubai who had video interviews with candidates to pilot his private jet, but still insisted on meeting the shortlisted ones face-to-face. Apparently, those interviews took exactly a few seconds each: all he needed was to see them in real life before making his choice.

It's because of the destructive power of a first impression that you simply have to do your preparation thoroughly. I strongly recommend a visit to the venue a day or two before the event to do a recce. Climb the stage or stand in the speaking area because it's important to familiarise yourself with the space. Are there any hidden ledges that you might trip over and how steep are the stairs? Clap your hands loudly in the space and listen to the acoustics. Does the sound reflect? What are the furnishings like? Soft carpets and curtains or tile floors and hard surfaces? There should be a balance between soft and hard surfaces to carry your voice sufficiently without having to use a microphone. If you do need a microphone, a sound check with the audio engineer is essential. Find out exactly how to turn the microphone on and off, if that's expected of you, and always do a practice run with the microphone even if you are a seasoned speaker.

Remember that what appears to be a relatively simple procedure during the rehearsal will feel totally different when you have three hundred pairs of eyes staring at you. Therefore, you need to make sure that your equipment is working one hundred percent. Even a small detail like new batteries for your screen clicker should be taken into account. Speakers need to be over-prepared because it helps to give you the extra confidence you need. Never be complacent, even if you have done it a hundred times, the hundred-and-first time might be the one time when the microphone battery runs out halfway through your presentation.

You are only as good as your last presentation – which simply means that you can never assume that you are beyond preparation.

WHICH ONE ARE YOU?

Are you the one who walks into the meeting room babbling away on his phone? The one who rushes in hardly noticing anyone else? The one who slips in as unobtrusively as possible, looking down and sliding into the first available chair or the one with no device in sight, shoulders back, chin up and making eye contact? The way you enter a meeting room or join a video conference can make or break you.

In her new book, *Presence*, Professor Amy Cuddy from Harvard Business School says people ask two questions in their minds when they see you for the first time: Can I trust this person? Can I respect this person?

And because all of us want to be perceived as both, we have to take extra care to come across as trustworthy and respectable. The Look (step one), the sound of your voice (step two) and your confidence (step three) all contribute to your overall presence – please handle it with care.

3

STEP THREE: DON'T WALK, STRIDE

"Never turn down the volume of who you are for anyone. When the world attempts to shush you, shame you, silence you, or tells you to 'act normal', please don't. Your genius is unique. Your chemistry is unrepeatable. We're on the planet for a relatively short amount of time. Don't waste any of it by hiding the truth of who you really are."
— MARIE FORLEO

You've learnt how to stand, how to gesture, how to prepare, how to rehearse and even how to produce a resonant voice, so why on earth are you still nervous? I'll tell you why. When you stand in front of all those people or see your face on a close up on a screen, you feel exposed.

What is the one thing that Amazon cannot deliver? The only thing that you've got that nobody can copy and paste? That cannot be bought online? The one thing that cannot be googled? Your personality. That is what makes you different from everybody else in the room. And that is what your audience wants, not your slick delivery of facts which they can google. The only thing that you can give them is you.

HOW?

Communication coaches will tell you: "*Just be yourself*." That is probably the most difficult thing to do. How does one give of yourself to a horde of strangers or maybe well-known colleagues or friends and family, when you have to stand up and discard your barriers, let your fences down, open the gate and let them see you?

It's exactly that – that feeling of nakedness, exposure, which makes us fearful. Those pairs of eyes focused on you, scrutinising you from the top of your head to the tips of your toes. That feeling that you are being judged, rejected or even ostracised. In a most interesting article in *Psychology Today*, Glen Croston Ph.D. author of 'The

Real Story of Risk' says the moment you are in the spotlight, the primal fear of being kicked out of the tribe sets in. You are fearful because you are facing this battle all by yourself – your group has deserted you. That is what causes glossophobia.

If you succeed in making the audience your tribe, your new group, you'll immediately feel 'at home'. Here's how to do it.

As soon as you manage to forget about yourself – you will be yourself.

BE YOURSELF

Being yourself is the secret to your success. Stop copying influencers because you don't want to be like everybody else. You don't want to look like them, act like them and, worst of all, talk like them. Instagram makes us decorate our houses the same way, wear the same outfits and cook the same meals. But when you stand up to speak, there is only one Sarah, one Phillip or one Connor – and that is the person we've come to listen to. Let your own true personality – your relaxed inner being – shine through the armour of pretence. Bare your soul and you will not believe the response you'll get from your audience.

Google provides information, entertainment and training, but it does not showcase the real face-to-face person. Your video version is not the same as your live performance – the person your audience gets to know when you are standing in front of them. That is the person I want you to be: the one who gives of himself; who thinks on his feet; who comes up with quips; who drops all pretence; who is not afraid to let his audience come close to him. And the way to do it is to be yourself.

Easier said than done? Indeed. You will not be able to do it if you allow fear or nerves to boycott you.

WHAT IS THE DEFINITION OF A GOOD SPEAKER?

> *"Don't give a speech: meet with your audience. Offer them information packaged by you personally. Let your personality shine through."*
> – BILL BRAND

The moment you shift your attention from you to them – that is the moment when you become a speaker, without saying a single word. The moment when you start paying attention instead of gaining attention. You can only be yourself if you stop thinking about yourself.

Speaking in front of people is not a case of: "*I am here, you are there, you shut up and listen to me.*" Move your focus from "*I came to deliver a speech*" to "*we're meeting to discuss; we're going to share ideas; the subject on the table is...*"

The moment you put your audience first, you're bound to get positive reaction, questions and comments. Hoorah! That is exactly what you need, because it opens the door to audience interaction and puts you on the road to becoming a world class Speaker.

HOW FEAR REARS ITS UGLY HEAD

When I'm nervous, I bite the inside of my lips and that's an ugly sight – especially on camera. Maybe you clench your fists, kick a leg, or there's a twitch – an eye, or your nose. I've even seen a nervous twitch of the ears. Whatever it is, it must go. Yes, of course we need to be more 'real', show our audiences ourselves warts and all, but I do believe that some camera training and a tiny bit of attention to detail will give you the edge – that confidence your followers will notice when they see you in action.

Here's my advice:

- Mount your camera or phone and video yourself, then sit back and look at it critically as though you're watching someone else. Watch it again and again and after the fifth or sixth time you will get some distance. Or ask somebody to critique it with you. Anything that distracts from what you are saying is wrong. Anything that catches your eye – clothing, hair in the face, makeup, jewellery and of course, any nervous twitch or movement – make a note of it and stop doing it. This is also an ideal way to discover your stop words such as *uhm, so, okay, you know what I mean* and *actually*.
- As we know by now, the camera tells it as it is: it accentuates everything. That uneven cuticle is going to look far worse on camera. Chipped nail varnish is not acceptable. Go for a manicure before your next video shoot – and that also applies to men. Have

your hair done and if your girlfriend's friend is a make-up artist, ask her about the best tips for covering up any blemishes because, believe me, on camera they are going to be highlighted.

■ And of course, also look critically at the backdrop: do you have enough depth behind you? Is the background uncluttered and does it enhance your message? We once shot a series of daily devotionals with a cool young pastor. His message on loneliness was shot in a bar at ten in the morning. We caught all the regulars, who had nothing else to do in the morning. The visuals said it all. Think creatively and let the scene do the talking.

Take time to prepare. Rehearse your content and, equally important, look the part.

LOOK INSIDE

How do you feel inside? Do you have the energy to get up, smile and face the music? Or are you simply going through the motions? You're in this job now and you simply have to make it work. Therefore, you jump on that Tube, endure the pushing and shoving and do your best to please your boss. Or attend one exhausting virtual meeting after the other, day in and day out.

But where's the joy? I'll tell you where the joy is – right inside of you, hidden under such thick layers of pretence that nobody can see it, least of all you! Be honest, do you enjoy life? Are you truly happy? If you can answer yes, you are one of the less than forty percent of the billions of people on this planet who are happy in their own skins. And there are people who are truly content with their lives – mostly older people who have made peace with their circumstances, found peace in their beliefs and are truly loved and understood. May you be one of them.

CONFIDENCE KILLERS

"You will amount to nothing!"
"You are pathetic."
"Why can't you be more like your brother?"
"Don't be stupid!"
"You're a real nuisance."

Parents and teachers can be some of the cruellest people on the face of the earth. Telling a child once that he is an imbecile – and once is enough for those words to be imprinted in the boy's mind for the rest of time – could result in an insecure human being with a tendency to succumb to addiction. Most of us have heard words to that effect at one time or another and, although they have not harmed us physically, they have surely set us back – sometimes more than we realise.

Another big confidence killer is circumstances – illness, depression, loneliness, emigration, losing a loved one, menopause – and as they say, the show must go on. Those are the times when one has to pick oneself up and just do it. If this should happen to you, I recommend that you take extra care to be fit and healthy. And don't be ashamed to cry. I once heard that tears represent the clean water that washes away the debris and waste in a river and enables it to flow again.

ARE YOU BEAUTIFUL?

If you are part of the sixty percent who are not totally content with their lives, you may want to begin thinking about yourself.

Answer these six questions:

- Are you attractive?
- Are you clever?
- Are you well-mannered?
- Are you educated?
- Are you experienced?
- Are you friendly?

If you could answer yes to only two of these questions, you have nearly a forty percent chance of standing out in a crowd and making an impression when you enter a room, which means you have an excellent foundation to build on.

Let's see what is inside of you – let's look for those building blocks to create the new you. The person who is going to lift up her chin, stand tall, look the world in the eye and speak up in such a way that everybody she addresses will put down their mobiles and listen.

Someone once said to me: everything you have done in your life, the good and the bad, turned you into the person you are today – and that is the person you should be proud of.

Our perception of ourselves is mostly far removed from reality. A lecturer once made the class do an interesting experiment. He asked us to draw the outline of our bodies with green chalk against a white wall and then go and stand against our own outlines. The girls all imagined their bodies bigger than they were and most of the guys saw themselves smaller than they were. It clearly proved that we don't see ourselves the way we really are. How strange and how true.

REBUILDING YOUR SELF-ESTEEM

This may seem superficial and frivolous, however, if you start searching for something nice to say to the next person you meet tomorrow – "*that colour really suits you; you have such a friendly smile; your report is to the point, well done*" – you'll not only make their confidence grow, but your view of yourself will improve dramatically. By experiencing how well people respond to your positive feedback you'll grow physically and mentally in stature. And before you know it, you will receive a compliment in return. The first block in building the new you.

WINNERS TAKE IT ALL

Surround yourself with positive, energetic, intelligent people who can inspire you to be your best. You must have certain people in your life who manage to totally drain you, who use up all your energy. When you say goodbye to them, you feel despondent, tired and even depressed. I think of them as vultures – all they do is to dig their claws into you and suck you dry. Why? Because they do not have any real happiness or fulfilment in their own lives. They thrive on other people's energy and they will act as your best friend only because you supply them with the fuel they need to survive.

These are the takers. And if you are a giver, you will end up feeding the taker until the day when you realise: hang on, what does he or she give me in return?

THE FIVE FINGER PRINCIPLE: WHAT'S–IN–IT–FOR–ME?

In business it's imperative to know what's it in for you before you enter into any deal. The same applies when you're communicating. Everyone

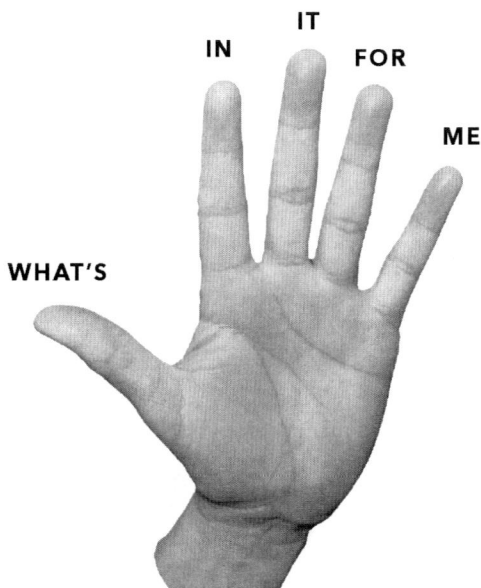

in the audience comes to the meeting or event with one thing on his or her mind: what can I gain from this?

As soon as you start giving your time, your energy, your expertise, you need to be sure that you are going to be rewarded. I'm not talking about participating in charity projects. Of course, you should invest in your community. The seeds that you sow will produce a golden harvest that not only enhances your profile but will make you a far better person. Those are the "I don't mind what's in it for me" moments, because what is in it for you, eventually, cannot be calculated in terms of pennies and pounds.

WHAT FILLS UP YOUR BISCUIT TIN?

If you feel drained at the end of the day, if you are the one who's making sacrifices, who always goes the second mile, then you're probably giving more than you receive. Whose fault is that? The mirror will tell you.

Have you heard the biscuit tin analogy? Imagine your day as a full biscuit tin. Every morning you should wake up with enough biscuits to hand out to those who openly ask for one, or to those whom you know would benefit from one. By midday, or even often before that, your biscuit tin is almost empty. Your energy is spent and you are beginning to run on empty. Establish what fills up your biscuit tin and do it! Once your tin is full, you'll be able to hand out biscuits. If not, you'll give and give and eventually end up in hospital – or maybe come off even worse.

To fill up your tin, you may need something as simple as recognition. When you send your husband out with a shopping list (after he has video-called you numerous times) and he finally brings back the spoils, you should leave everything you're doing and join him in the kitchen where he's busy unpacking the items and placing them in a neat row on the counter. The hunter is home. You will fill his biscuit tin to the brim if you say: "*Darling, you're so clever. That's exactly what I wanted. Thank you so much.*"

And he will fill up your biscuit tin, when you have spent two hours in the bedroom, choosing your outfit, doing your hair, taking time with your make-up and when you appear, he pretends to faint. Most of us are in a constant mode of giving: to our partners, our children, our bosses, our friends and family. It never stops. When was the last time that you thought only of yourself? Is it selfish? No. Survival? Yes.

To get back to the five-finger principle, it's important to spot those takers who target you to tap your brain, use your time, swallow your energy to further their own enterprises. Be careful of those leeches who say: "*I have this amazing concept…*" You don't need concepts; you probably have a thousand concepts already. You need people who recognise your experience and skills and are prepared to pay a consultation fee for your time. Those are the people for whom you'll walk the extra mile – and, as strange as it may seem, you'll also have some biscuits left.

AM I A GOOD SPEAKER?

> "*There are always three speeches for every one you gave. The one you practised, the one you gave, and the one you wish you gave.*"
> —DALE CARNEGIE

This is a quote by the famous American author, Dale Carnegie who wrote *How to Win Friends and Influence People*. He is so right! Do you ever feel that the presentation you gave wasn't good enough? That it could have been smoother, more arresting or more commanding? Stop worrying about it. Once it's done, it's over. Step away from it, learn from it or bask in your success, but never dwell on it. Rather begin to look forward to the next one. And know that it will be better in every way because, by having a video taken of your speech, you'll be able to recognise the weak points and turn them into the strong points the next time around.

WINNING WORDS

Here is something very important which will make you feel more empowered when you prepare for your next public performance, something which I refer to as 'winning words'. The words you choose when you speak have a major impact on how you come across. Let's take a simple everyday expression such as "*I think*". The very essence of the term 'think' points to something that is not established, something that's fluid, unfinished, not proven and certainly not credible or trustworthy. Remember what Professor Amy Cuddy said? When people meet you for the first time, they ask two questions: can I respect this person? Can I trust this person?

Let's replace 'think' with a winning word, let's say 'believe': "*I believe I'm the right person for this position.*" Or "*I believe the best solution is to devise a strategy which addresses the problem and not the symptoms.*" Use 'committed' instead of 'will'. For example, "*I will be able to handle it*" becomes "*I'm committed to succeed*". Exchange 'I will try' with 'I know'. "*I know I can beat him*" sounds more convincing than "*I'll try to beat him in the next round*".

Life expects us to take part in the struggle for survival where dog eats dog, where each one of us has to fight for a place in the sun. It's not easy. Therefore, you have to stand tall, look the world in the eye and use your voice, your hands and your whole body to make people take notice.

Here's something important for anybody who feels that they are not being heard. Become more assertive. Try to begin your sentences in future with: I want, I need, I require, or I demand. Even if you never say "*I demand*", it's reassuring to know that you have that phrase up your sleeve the next time a call centre agent keeps you waiting for thirty minutes and then puts you through to his colleague whom you've already spoken to! That is when "I demand" seems appropriate.

YOU ARE READY

"Success is never accidental."
–JACK DORSEY

You've embarked on the exciting journey of finding your voice. You know how to stand, how to walk and how to enter a room or join a meeting, but maybe there is still a tiny bit of hesitation, a feeling of "will I remember everything I've learned when it's my turn to speak?".

No, you won't. And I don't want you to try and think of all the do's and don'ts. I want you to relax and enjoy it. Once you've managed that, you'd be surprised at how many of these tips have become part of your DNA... part of your poem.

Grab the opportunity with both hands. I know you can do it.

RECOMMENDED READING LIST

Mehrabian, Albert; *Silent Messages*; Academia. edu, 1971

C. David Mortensen, Kenneth K. Sereno; *Advances in Communication Research*; Harper & Row, 1973

Gladwell, Malcolm; *The Tipping Point*; CreateSpace, 2017

Croston, Glenn; *Real Story of Risk: Adventures in a Hazardous World*; Prometheus, 2012.

Cuddy, Amy Joy; *Presence*; Little, Brown Book Group, 2015

Stanislavski, Constantin; *An Actor Prepares*; A&C Black, 2013

Day, Elizabeth; *How to Fail*; 4th Estate, 2019

Chaney, Lisa; *Chanel, An Intimate Life*; Penguin, 2012

Carnegie, Dale; *How to Win Friends and Influence People*; Simon & Schuster, 2006

Taylor, David; *The Naked Leader*; Capstone Publishing Ltd, 2002

ABOUT THE AUTHOR

Mariette's interest in public speaking was sparked at the age of three when her father, who was an accomplished Toastmaster, encouraged his children to find their own voices. From running a speech and drama studio to performing on television, radio and stage, Mariette is now applying her experience to coach business professionals internationally. She has received the South African Broadcasting Award for Children Storytelling, the Best Actress Award for various student productions and for a musical, Night in the Karoo (Karoonag). She was the co-author of Jip, a series of stories for the youth and she produced a ballet edutainment video series of Coppélia which includes the complete ballet performance, The Sandman's Tale (a simplified version for younger viewers) a ballet master-class and interviews. Her video series on performance coaching has won wide acclaim.